# Table of Contents

# Chapter 1: Introduction to Artificial General Intelligence (AGI)

## What is AGI?

Artificial General Intelligence (AGI) refers to a form of artificial intelligence that possesses the ability to understand, learn, and apply knowledge across a wide range of tasks and domains, much like a human being. Unlike narrow AI systems, which are designed to excel at specific tasks, AGI aims to replicate the general cognitive abilities of humans, such as reasoning, problem-solving, and abstract thinking. The ultimate goal of AGI research is to create machines that can perform any intellectual task that a human can, and potentially surpass human intelligence in the future.

AGI represents a significant leap forward in the field of artificial intelligence, as it has the potential to revolutionize industries, improve efficiency, and solve complex problems that have eluded human solutions. However, the development of AGI also raises important ethical considerations, such as the implications of creating machines that are capable of independent thought and decision-making. There are concerns about the impact of AGI on society, including issues related to privacy, security, and job displacement. It is essential for researchers, policymakers, and industry leaders to address these ethical considerations proactively to ensure that AGI is developed and deployed responsibly.

In addition to ethical considerations, the development of AGI also raises questions about regulation and governance. As AGI systems become more sophisticated and autonomous, there is a need for robust regulatory frameworks to ensure that these systems are used in a safe and ethical manner. This includes guidelines for data privacy, transparency, accountability, and oversight. Governments and international organizations must work together to establish global standards for the development and deployment of AGI to prevent misuse and ensure that the benefits of AGI are shared equitably among all people.

Technical challenges are another key aspect of AGI that researchers must address. Building a machine that can replicate the complex cognitive abilities of humans requires advancements in a wide range of fields, including neuroscience, computer science, mathematics, and psychology. Researchers must develop new algorithms, architectures, and models that can handle the complexities of human-like intelligence, such as reasoning, creativity, and emotional intelligence. Overcoming these technical challenges will require collaboration and innovation across disciplines to unlock the full potential of AGI.

Finally, the economic impact of AGI cannot be overlooked. The widespread adoption of AGI has the potential to disrupt industries, create new job opportunities, and reshape the global economy. While AGI has the potential to increase productivity and drive innovation, it also raises concerns about job displacement and income inequality. It is essential for policymakers and industry leaders to develop strategies to mitigate the negative economic impacts of AGI, such as reskilling programs, social safety nets, and policies that promote inclusive growth. By addressing these economic challenges proactively, society can harness the full potential of AGI to create a more prosperous and equitable future for all.

## Importance of AGI

In the world of artificial intelligence (AI), there is a growing interest and excitement surrounding the development of Artificial General Intelligence (AGI). AGI represents a significant milestone in the field of AI, as it aims to create machines that can perform any intellectual task that a human can. The importance of AGI cannot be understated, as it has the potential to revolutionize countless industries and fundamentally change the way we live and work.

One of the key reasons why AGI is so important is its potential to solve some of the most complex and pressing problems facing society today. From climate change to healthcare to poverty, AGI has the potential to provide innovative solutions that could have a profound impact on the world. By harnessing the power of AGI, researchers and scientists can tackle these challenges in ways that were previously unimaginable, leading to a brighter and more sustainable future for all.

Additionally, AGI has the potential to greatly enhance human capabilities and improve our quality of life. By automating mundane and repetitive tasks, AGI can free up time and resources for individuals to focus on more meaningful and creative pursuits. This can lead to increased productivity, innovation, and overall well-being, ultimately creating a more efficient and fulfilling society.

Furthermore, AGI has the potential to drive economic growth and create new opportunities for businesses and industries. By leveraging the power of AGI, companies can streamline operations, increase efficiency, and develop new products and services that were previously impossible. This can lead to increased competitiveness, job creation, and overall economic prosperity, benefiting both businesses and individuals alike.

In conclusion, the importance of AGI cannot be overstated. From solving complex societal problems to enhancing human capabilities to driving economic growth, AGI has the potential to revolutionize countless aspects of our lives. As we continue to make progress in the development of AGI, it is crucial that we approach this technology with careful consideration and foresight, ensuring that we harness its power for the greater good of humanity.

## Historical Development of AGI

The historical development of Artificial General Intelligence (AGI) can be traced back to the early days of computing when researchers began to explore the idea of creating machines that could mimic human intelligence. One of the key milestones in the development of AGI was the creation of the first neural networks in the 1950s, which laid the foundation for modern artificial intelligence technologies.

In the 1960s and 1970s, researchers began to develop expert systems that could perform specific tasks at a level comparable to human experts. This marked the beginning of the era of narrow AI, where machines were designed to excel in specific domains but lacked the ability to generalize their knowledge to new tasks. It was not until the 1980s and 1990s that researchers began to explore the concept of AGI in earnest, with the goal of creating machines that could learn and adapt in a manner similar to humans.

The turn of the millennium saw significant advancements in the field of AGI, with the development of deep learning algorithms that could automatically learn from large amounts of data. This led to breakthroughs in areas such as speech recognition, image classification, and natural language processing, bringing AI technologies closer to achieving human-level intelligence.

In recent years, there has been a growing recognition of the ethical considerations surrounding the development of AGI, with concerns about the potential impact on jobs, privacy, and security. This has led to calls for greater regulation and governance of AI technologies to ensure that they are developed and deployed responsibly.

Despite the challenges and uncertainties that lie ahead, the continued progress in the field of AGI holds the promise of revolutionizing industries, transforming societies, and reshaping the way we live and work. As we navigate the complex landscape of artificial intelligence, it is essential to stay informed, engaged, and proactive in shaping the future of AGI for the benefit of all.

# Chapter 2: Development Progress of AGI

## Current State of AGI Research

The current state of AGI research is a rapidly evolving landscape that is constantly pushing the boundaries of what is possible in the field of artificial intelligence. Researchers around the world are working tirelessly to develop systems that can not only perform specific tasks but also demonstrate human-like cognitive abilities such as reasoning, learning, and problem-solving. While significant progress has been made in recent years, true AGI still remains a distant goal that requires further exploration and innovation.

One of the key challenges in AGI research is the development of algorithms and architectures that can support general intelligence across a wide range of tasks and domains. Current approaches often rely on deep learning models that excel at specific tasks but struggle to generalize beyond the training data they have been exposed to. Researchers are actively exploring new paradigms such as reinforcement learning, evolutionary algorithms, and neuro-symbolic systems to overcome these limitations and create more robust and adaptable AGI systems.

Ethical considerations also play a crucial role in shaping the direction of AGI research. As artificial intelligence becomes increasingly integrated into society, questions around privacy, bias, accountability, and transparency must be carefully considered to ensure that AGI systems are developed and deployed in a responsible and ethical manner. Researchers are actively engaging with policymakers, industry stakeholders, and the public to address these concerns and establish guidelines for the ethical development and use of AGI technology.

Regulation and governance are another important aspect of AGI research that must be carefully navigated to ensure the responsible and safe deployment of AI systems. As AGI technology becomes more advanced, there is a growing need for clear guidelines and frameworks to govern its development and use. Policymakers and regulatory bodies are working to establish standards and regulations that promote innovation while safeguarding against potential risks and unintended consequences of AGI technology.

Overall, the current state of AGI research is characterized by rapid advancements, complex challenges, and a growing awareness of the ethical and regulatory considerations that must be addressed. As researchers continue to push the boundaries of artificial intelligence, it is essential that they remain vigilant in addressing these challenges and working towards the development of AGI systems that are not only powerful and intelligent but also safe, ethical, and beneficial for society as a whole.

## Challenges in Developing AGI

Developing Artificial General Intelligence (AGI) poses numerous challenges that must be overcome in order to successfully create a machine that can perform any intellectual task that a human can. One of the main challenges in developing AGI is the complexity of human cognition. Human intelligence is incredibly intricate and multifaceted, making it difficult to replicate in a machine. Researchers must carefully study and understand the various aspects of human intelligence in order to create a truly autonomous and intelligent machine.

Another challenge in developing AGI is the lack of a unified theory of intelligence. While there are many theories and models of intelligence, none have been universally accepted as the definitive explanation of how intelligence works. This lack of consensus makes it difficult for researchers to determine the best approach to developing AGI. Without a clear understanding of intelligence, progress in creating a truly intelligent machine is hindered.

Additionally, ethical considerations present a significant challenge in developing AGI. As machines become more intelligent and autonomous, questions about the ethical implications of creating machines that can think and act like humans arise. Issues such as machine ethics, rights, and responsibilities must be carefully considered in order to ensure that AGI is developed in a responsible and ethical manner.

Regulation and governance also pose challenges in the development of AGI. As AGI becomes more advanced, concerns about the potential risks and consequences of creating machines with human-level intelligence increase. It is essential for governments and regulatory bodies to establish guidelines and regulations to ensure the safe and responsible development of AGI.

Finally, technical challenges such as scalability, robustness, and interpretability must be addressed in order to create a truly intelligent machine. AGI systems must be able to handle large amounts of data, adapt to new environments, and provide explanations for their decisions in order to be truly intelligent. Overcoming these technical challenges is essential for the successful development of AGI.

## Future Prospects of AGI

The future prospects of Artificial General Intelligence (AGI) are both exciting and uncertain. As we continue to make technological advancements in the field of AI, the possibility of achieving AGI becomes more realistic. AGI has the potential to revolutionize industries, improve efficiency in various sectors, and enhance our daily lives in ways we never thought possible.

One of the key future prospects of AGI is its impact on job automation. With the ability to perform a wide range of tasks that currently require human intelligence, AGI has the potential to automate many jobs across different industries. While this may lead to increased efficiency and productivity, it also raises concerns about potential job displacement and the need for retraining the workforce for new roles.

Another prospect of AGI lies in its potential to solve complex problems that are currently beyond human capabilities. AGI could revolutionize scientific research, medicine, and other fields by processing vast amounts of data and generating insights and solutions at a speed and scale that humans cannot match. This could lead to major breakthroughs in areas such as drug discovery, climate change mitigation, and space exploration.

Ethical considerations surrounding AGI are also a crucial aspect of its future prospects. As AGI becomes more advanced and capable of autonomous decision-making, questions arise about the ethical implications of its actions. Ensuring that AGI is developed and used responsibly, with proper safeguards in place to prevent harm to society, will be essential in shaping a positive future for this technology.

Regulation and governance of AGI are also important factors to consider in its future prospects. As AGI becomes more widespread and integrated into various systems and industries, there will be a need for clear guidelines and regulations to ensure its safe and ethical use. Governments and international organizations will need to work together to establish standards and protocols for the development and deployment of AGI.

Overall, the future prospects of AGI hold immense promise for transforming our world in ways we have yet to imagine. By addressing the challenges and ethical considerations associated with this technology, we can harness its full potential to create a better future for all of humanity.

# Chapter 3: Ethical Considerations in AGI

## Moral Implications of AGI

The development of Artificial General Intelligence (AGI) raises numerous moral implications that must be carefully considered. One of the main concerns is the potential for AGI to surpass human intelligence, leading to questions about the rights and responsibilities of these advanced machines. As AGI becomes more autonomous and capable of making decisions on its own, we must grapple with the ethical implications of granting such entities rights and ensuring they act in accordance with moral principles.

Another moral consideration surrounding AGI is the potential for biases to be encoded into the systems during their development. If not carefully monitored, these biases could lead to discriminatory actions by AGI towards certain groups of people. It is essential that developers take steps to mitigate bias in AGI systems to ensure they act in a fair and just manner.

Furthermore, the impact of AGI on the job market and economy raises ethical questions about the distribution of wealth and opportunities. As AGI becomes more capable of performing tasks traditionally done by humans, there is a risk of widespread job displacement. It is crucial to consider how society will address these challenges and ensure that the benefits of AGI are shared equitably among all members of society.

Additionally, the use of AGI in warfare and surveillance presents significant moral implications. The potential for AGI to be used in military applications raises concerns about the ethical use of such technology and the potential for harm to civilians. It is essential for policymakers to establish regulations and guidelines to ensure that AGI is used ethically and responsibly in these contexts.

In conclusion, the moral implications of AGI are vast and complex, requiring careful consideration and ethical reflection. As we continue to develop and deploy AGI systems, it is essential that we prioritize ethical considerations to ensure that these advanced machines act in accordance with our values and principles. By addressing these moral implications proactively, we can harness the full potential of AGI while minimizing the risks and ensuring a positive impact on society.

## Risks and Benefits of AGI

In the world of Artificial General Intelligence (AGI), there are both risks and benefits that come with the development and implementation of this powerful technology. Understanding these risks and benefits is crucial for ensuring that AGI is used in a responsible and ethical manner.

One of the main benefits of AGI is its potential to revolutionize industries and improve efficiency in ways that were previously unimaginable. AGI has the ability to automate tasks that were once time-consuming and labor-intensive, freeing up human workers to focus on more creative and strategic endeavors. This can lead to increased productivity and innovation in a wide range of fields, from healthcare to manufacturing to finance.

However, the rapid advancement of AGI also comes with a number of risks that must be carefully considered. One of the biggest concerns surrounding AGI is the potential for job displacement as automation becomes more prevalent. As AGI becomes more sophisticated and capable of performing complex tasks, there is a risk that many jobs could be replaced by machines, leading to widespread unemployment and economic instability.

There are also ethical considerations to take into account when it comes to the development and use of AGI. Questions of privacy, security, and accountability must be addressed to ensure that AGI is used in a way that respects human rights and values. There is also the risk of AGI being used for malicious purposes, such as autonomous weapons or surveillance systems, which could have devastating consequences if not properly regulated.

In order to mitigate these risks and maximize the benefits of AGI, it is crucial that regulations and governance structures are put in place to ensure that AGI is developed and used responsibly. This includes establishing clear guidelines for how AGI can be used, as well as mechanisms for oversight and accountability to prevent misuse. By taking a proactive approach to regulation and governance, we can help ensure that AGI is used in a way that benefits society as a whole.

Overall, the risks and benefits of AGI are complex and multifaceted, requiring careful consideration and thoughtful planning to navigate successfully. By understanding these risks and benefits and taking proactive steps to address them, we can harness the full potential of AGI while minimizing the potential negative consequences.

## Ethical Guidelines for AGI Development

In the quest to develop Artificial General Intelligence (AGI), it is crucial to adhere to ethical guidelines to ensure that the technology is aligned with human values and interests. Ethical considerations in AGI development are essential to prevent potential harms and misuse of the technology. This subchapter will outline key ethical guidelines that should be followed in the development of AGI.

One of the primary ethical guidelines for AGI development is transparency. Developers should strive to make their algorithms and decision-making processes transparent to ensure accountability and to build trust with users. Transparent AGI systems are more likely to be accepted by society and less likely to be perceived as a threat.

Another important ethical consideration is fairness and bias mitigation. AGI systems should be designed to be fair and unbiased, taking into account the diverse perspectives and needs of different user groups. Developers should actively work to identify and mitigate biases in their algorithms to prevent discriminatory outcomes.

Privacy and data protection are also crucial ethical guidelines for AGI development. Developers should prioritize the protection of user data and privacy rights, ensuring that AGI systems comply with relevant data protection laws and regulations. By respecting user privacy, developers can build trust with users and ensure the ethical use of AGI technology.

In addition, developers should consider the potential social impact of AGI technology and work to minimize negative consequences. Ethical guidelines should include considerations for the impact of AGI on employment, inequality, and societal structures. Developers should engage with stakeholders and experts to anticipate and address potential social challenges posed by AGI technology.

Overall, ethical guidelines for AGI development should prioritize transparency, fairness, privacy, and social impact. By adhering to these guidelines, developers can ensure that AGI technology is developed and deployed in a responsible and ethical manner, benefiting society as a whole.

# Chapter 4: Regulation and Governance of AGI

## International Regulations on AGI

As the development of Artificial General Intelligence (AGI) continues to progress, the need for international regulations on AGI becomes increasingly important. With the potential for AGI to revolutionize industries and society as a whole, it is crucial to establish a framework that ensures its safe and ethical deployment. International regulations on AGI aim to address various concerns such as data privacy, security, transparency, accountability, and the impact of AGI on jobs and the economy.

One of the key considerations in the development of international regulations on AGI is the need for collaboration among nations. AGI is a global technology that transcends borders, and thus requires a unified approach to regulation. International cooperation is essential to ensure that regulations are harmonized across countries and that there are mechanisms in place for enforcing compliance.

Another important aspect of international regulations on AGI is the need for ethical guidelines. As AGI systems become more sophisticated and autonomous, there is a growing concern about the potential for these systems to make decisions that could have unintended consequences. Ethical guidelines can help ensure that AGI systems are developed and deployed in a way that aligns with human values and respects fundamental rights.

In addition to ethical considerations, international regulations on AGI also need to address technical challenges. AGI systems are complex and can be difficult to understand, making it challenging to regulate them effectively. Regulations need to take into account the unique characteristics of AGI systems and ensure that they are designed and operated in a way that minimizes risks and maximizes benefits.

Overall, international regulations on AGI play a crucial role in shaping the future of this transformative technology. By establishing a framework that addresses ethical, technical, and economic considerations, we can ensure that AGI is developed and deployed in a way that benefits society as a whole. Collaboration among nations, the establishment of ethical guidelines, and addressing technical challenges are all essential components of effective international regulations on AGI.

## National Policies on AGI

National policies on Artificial General Intelligence (AGI) play a crucial role in shaping the development and deployment of this transformative technology. Different countries have taken varying approaches to regulating AGI, reflecting their unique political, social, and economic contexts. In this subchapter, we will explore some of the key national policies on AGI and their implications for the global landscape.

One of the leading countries in AGI research and development is the United States. The US government has adopted a relatively hands-off approach to regulating AGI, preferring to rely on industry self-regulation and voluntary guidelines. This approach has allowed American companies to take the lead in developing AGI technologies, but it has also raised concerns about the potential lack of oversight and accountability in the industry.

In contrast, countries like China have taken a more proactive stance on AGI regulation. The Chinese government has invested heavily in AGI research and development, but it has also implemented strict regulations to ensure the responsible and ethical use of the technology. This includes guidelines on data privacy, algorithm transparency, and the ethical treatment of AI systems.

European countries have also been active in shaping national policies on AGI. The European Union, in particular, has proposed comprehensive regulations on AI, including AGI, to protect consumer rights and promote ethical standards. These regulations include requirements for algorithmic transparency, accountability mechanisms, and safeguards against bias and discrimination.

Overall, national policies on AGI reflect a complex interplay of technological progress, ethical considerations, economic interests, and societal values. As AGI continues to advance, it will be crucial for policymakers to strike a balance between promoting innovation and safeguarding the public interest. By studying and understanding the different approaches taken by countries around the world, we can better navigate the challenges and opportunities presented by this groundbreaking technology.

## Governance Models for AGI

As the development of Artificial General Intelligence (AGI) progresses, the need for effective governance models becomes increasingly apparent. AGI has the potential to revolutionize industries, reshape economies, and even impact the very fabric of society. Therefore, it is crucial to establish frameworks that ensure its development and deployment are done in a responsible and ethical manner.

One governance model that has gained traction in recent years is the idea of a Global AI Council. This council would be comprised of experts from various fields, including ethics, law, technology, and economics, who would work together to establish guidelines and regulations for the development and deployment of AGI. By bringing together diverse perspectives, the council could help ensure that AGI is developed in a way that benefits society as a whole.

Another governance model that has been proposed is the idea of a decentralized governance system. In this model, decisions about AGI development and deployment would be made by a network of stakeholders, including researchers, policymakers, industry leaders, and members of the public. This approach aims to distribute power and decision-making authority more evenly, reducing the risk of AGI being controlled by a small group of individuals or organizations.

A third governance model that is gaining attention is the concept of AI Impact Assessments. Similar to environmental impact assessments, these assessments would evaluate the potential social, economic, and ethical impacts of AGI before it is deployed. By conducting thorough assessments, policymakers can better understand the risks and benefits of AGI and make informed decisions about its development and regulation.

In conclusion, governance models for AGI are essential for ensuring that this powerful technology is developed and deployed responsibly. By establishing frameworks such as Global AI Councils, decentralized governance systems, and AI Impact Assessments, we can work towards harnessing the potential of AGI while minimizing its risks. It is crucial that these governance models are developed in collaboration with a diverse range of stakeholders to ensure that AGI benefits society as a whole.

# Chapter 5: Technical Challenges in AGI

## Building General Intelligence

Building General Intelligence is a complex and multifaceted process that involves a wide range of disciplines, including computer science, neuroscience, psychology, and philosophy. In order to create truly intelligent machines that can perform a wide range of tasks and adapt to new situations, researchers must draw on insights from these diverse fields and develop new methods and algorithms that can mimic the capabilities of the human brain.

One of the key challenges in building general intelligence is developing algorithms that can learn from experience and generalize across different tasks and domains. Traditional machine learning algorithms are often limited in their ability to generalize beyond the specific tasks they were trained on, requiring extensive hand-tuning and retraining when faced with new challenges. In contrast, truly intelligent systems should be able to adapt and learn from new experiences in a flexible and autonomous manner.

Another important aspect of building general intelligence is understanding the underlying principles of cognition and perception. By studying how the human brain processes information and makes decisions, researchers can gain insights into the fundamental mechanisms of intelligence and develop new algorithms and architectures that can replicate these processes in artificial systems. This interdisciplinary approach is crucial for advancing the field of artificial general intelligence and creating machines that can think, reason, and learn in a human-like manner.

Ethical considerations also play a critical role in the development of general intelligence. As intelligent machines become more advanced and autonomous, it is important to consider the ethical implications of their actions and ensure that they are designed and used in a responsible and ethical manner. This includes addressing potential risks and challenges such as bias, privacy concerns, and the impact of automation on the job market.

In conclusion, building general intelligence is a complex and challenging task that requires a multidisciplinary approach, a deep understanding of cognitive processes, and a strong focus on ethics and responsibility. By drawing on insights from a wide range of fields and developing new algorithms and architectures that can mimic the capabilities of the human brain, researchers can make significant progress towards creating truly intelligent machines that can adapt to new challenges and contribute to a better future for humanity.

## Overcoming Bias in AGI

Artificial General Intelligence (AGI) holds the potential to revolutionize industries, improve efficiency, and enhance our daily lives. However, one of the key challenges in developing AGI is overcoming bias. Bias in AI systems can lead to discriminatory outcomes, perpetuate stereotypes, and reinforce existing inequalities. In order to ensure that AGI benefits society as a whole, it is crucial to address and mitigate bias in the development process.

One way to overcome bias in AGI is through diverse and inclusive data sets. By including a wide range of perspectives and experiences in the training data, developers can help mitigate bias and ensure that the AGI system reflects the diversity of the real world. Additionally, using techniques such as data augmentation and adversarial training can help expose and eliminate biases in the data set.

Another approach to overcoming bias in AGI is through transparency and explainability. By making the decision-making process of AGI systems more transparent, developers can identify and address biases that may be present in the algorithms. Additionally, providing explanations for the recommendations and decisions made by AGI systems can help users better understand and trust the technology.

Ethical considerations also play a crucial role in overcoming bias in AGI. Developers must consider the potential impact of their technology on individuals and society as a whole, and take steps to mitigate any harmful consequences. By incorporating ethical guidelines and principles into the design and development process, developers can ensure that AGI is used in a responsible and equitable manner.

Regulation and governance are also essential for overcoming bias in AGI. Governments and regulatory bodies must establish guidelines and standards for the development and deployment of AGI systems, in order to ensure that they are fair, transparent, and accountable. By implementing regulations that address bias and discrimination, policymakers can help foster a more inclusive and equitable future for AGI.

## Ensuring Safety in AGI Systems

Safety is paramount when it comes to the development and deployment of Artificial General Intelligence (AGI) systems. Ensuring that AGI systems are safe and secure is crucial to prevent any potential harm or unintended consequences. In this subchapter, we will explore some key strategies and best practices for ensuring safety in AGI systems.

One important aspect of ensuring safety in AGI systems is robust testing and validation procedures. AGI systems should undergo rigorous testing to identify and address any potential vulnerabilities or weaknesses. This includes testing the system's behavior in various scenarios and edge cases to ensure that it performs reliably and predictably.

Another crucial factor in ensuring safety in AGI systems is transparency and explainability. AGI systems should be designed in such a way that their decisions and actions can be easily understood and explained. This not only helps to build trust in the system but also allows for easier identification and resolution of any potential safety issues.

Furthermore, implementing proper safeguards and fail-safes is essential for ensuring safety in AGI systems. These safeguards can include mechanisms for detecting and preventing harmful actions, as well as protocols for shutting down the system in case of emergencies. Additionally, ensuring that AGI systems are secure from external threats such as hacking or malicious attacks is also critical for ensuring safety.

In conclusion, ensuring safety in AGI systems is a multi-faceted challenge that requires a combination of robust testing, transparency, safeguards, and security measures. By following best practices and implementing proper safety protocols, we can mitigate the risks associated with AGI systems and ensure that they contribute positively to society. It is essential for developers, policymakers, and other stakeholders to work together to address these safety concerns and ensure a safe and secure future for AGI technologies.

# Chapter 6: Economic Impact of AGI

## Job Displacement by AGI

As Artificial General Intelligence (AGI) continues to advance rapidly, one of the major concerns that arises is the potential for job displacement. AGI has the capability to perform tasks that were previously only possible for humans, which means that many jobs currently held by humans could be at risk. This subchapter will explore the various ways in which AGI could lead to job displacement and the potential implications for society.

One of the main reasons why AGI could lead to job displacement is its ability to perform tasks more efficiently and accurately than humans. AGI systems are capable of processing vast amounts of data at incredible speeds, which means that they can complete tasks in a fraction of the time it would take a human to do the same job. As a result, many industries could see a significant decrease in the need for human workers, leading to widespread job displacement.

Another factor that could contribute to job displacement by AGI is the potential for automation. AGI systems have the ability to automate a wide range of tasks, from simple data entry to complex decision-making processes. This could lead to a significant reduction in the need for human workers in many industries, as companies could rely on AGI systems to perform these tasks more efficiently and cost-effectively.

The implications of job displacement by AGI are far-reaching and could have a significant impact on society as a whole. Not only could it lead to widespread unemployment and economic instability, but it could also exacerbate existing inequalities in the workforce. Those who are able to adapt to the new demands of the job market may thrive, while others could find themselves left behind, struggling to find employment in an increasingly automated world.

In order to address the potential for job displacement by AGI, it will be essential for policymakers, businesses, and society as a whole to work together to develop strategies for retraining and reskilling workers. This will be crucial in ensuring that those who are displaced by AGI are able to find new opportunities in the workforce and continue to contribute to society. By taking proactive measures to address the challenges of job displacement by AGI, we can help to mitigate the negative impacts and ensure a more equitable and sustainable future for all.

## Opportunities Created by AGI

Artificial General Intelligence (AGI) has the potential to create numerous opportunities across various industries and sectors. One of the most significant opportunities created by AGI is the ability to automate repetitive and mundane tasks, freeing up human workers to focus on more creative and strategic work. This can lead to increased productivity and efficiency in businesses, ultimately driving economic growth.

Furthermore, AGI can also revolutionize healthcare by enabling more accurate diagnoses and personalized treatment plans. With the ability to process vast amounts of data and identify patterns that human doctors might miss, AGI has the potential to save countless lives and improve overall health outcomes. Additionally, AGI can be used to develop new drugs and treatment methods at a much faster pace, accelerating medical advancements.

In the field of education, AGI can provide personalized learning experiences for students, catering to their individual needs and learning styles. This can help bridge the gap in educational disparities and ensure that every student has access to quality education. AGI can also assist teachers in grading assignments and providing feedback, allowing them to focus on mentoring and guiding students rather than administrative tasks.

Moreover, AGI can be leveraged in the field of cybersecurity to detect and prevent cyber threats in real-time. By analyzing vast amounts of data and identifying potential vulnerabilities, AGI can significantly enhance the security of digital systems and networks. This can help protect sensitive information and prevent cyber attacks, safeguarding businesses and individuals from potential harm.

Overall, the opportunities created by AGI are vast and diverse, spanning across various industries and sectors. As AGI continues to advance and evolve, it is crucial to harness its potential for the greater good of society, while also addressing ethical considerations and ensuring responsible development and deployment. By leveraging the opportunities created by AGI, we can unlock new possibilities and drive innovation in ways we never thought possible.

## Economic Implications of AGI Adoption

As Artificial General Intelligence (AGI) continues to progress and evolve, the economic implications of its adoption are becoming increasingly significant. The integration of AGI into various industries and sectors has the potential to revolutionize the way businesses operate, ultimately leading to increased efficiency, productivity, and profitability. However, this adoption also raises concerns about potential job displacement, income inequality, and overall economic stability.

One of the key economic implications of AGI adoption is its impact on the labor market. As AGI technology becomes more advanced, it has the potential to automate a wide range of tasks and jobs currently performed by humans. This automation could lead to significant job displacement in certain industries, particularly those that rely heavily on routine and repetitive tasks. As a result, there is a growing concern about the potential loss of jobs and the need for retraining and upskilling programs to help displaced workers transition to new roles.

On the flip side, the adoption of AGI also has the potential to create new job opportunities in emerging fields such as AI development, data science, and machine learning. These new roles will require specialized skills and expertise, creating demand for workers with technical knowledge and experience in AGI technologies. Additionally, the increased efficiency and productivity brought about by AGI adoption can lead to economic growth and expansion in industries that embrace these technologies.

Another important economic implication of AGI adoption is its potential impact on income inequality. As AGI technology becomes more prevalent, there is a risk that the benefits of automation and increased productivity will not be evenly distributed. Wealthier individuals and corporations may capture a larger share of the economic gains from AGI adoption, leading to further income inequality and disparities in wealth distribution. This could have far-reaching consequences for social stability and economic growth if not addressed through appropriate policies and regulations.

In conclusion, the adoption of AGI has the potential to bring about significant economic changes and disruptions in various industries and sectors. While the integration of AGI technologies can lead to increased efficiency, productivity, and economic growth, it also raises concerns about job displacement, income inequality, and overall economic stability. As we continue to navigate the complexities of AGI adoption, it will be crucial for policymakers, businesses, and society as a whole to consider the economic implications and take proactive steps to ensure that the benefits of AGI adoption are shared equitably and sustainably.

# Chapter 7: Conclusion

## Summary of Key Points

In this subchapter, we will summarize the key points covered in this comprehensive guide to Artificial General Intelligence (AGI). AGI refers to machines that have the ability to perform any intellectual task that a human can do.

First and foremost, we discussed the development progress of AGI. While significant advancements have been made in the field of AI, true AGI still remains a distant goal. Researchers are working tirelessly to build machines that can learn, reason, and adapt to new situations in a way that mimics human intelligence.

Next, we delved into the ethical considerations surrounding AGI. As machines become more intelligent, questions arise about the implications of giving machines the ability to make autonomous decisions. Issues such as privacy, bias, and job displacement must be carefully considered as we move forward in the development of AGI.

Regulation and governance of AGI are also crucial topics that were covered in this guide. It is essential to establish guidelines and regulations to ensure that AGI is developed and used responsibly. Without proper oversight, there is the potential for misuse and unintended consequences.

Technical challenges in the development of AGI were also discussed in detail. From creating machines that can understand natural language to developing algorithms that can learn from limited data, there are numerous obstacles that must be overcome in order to achieve true AGI.

Finally, we explored the economic impact of AGI. While AGI has the potential to revolutionize industries and improve efficiency, there are concerns about job displacement and income inequality. It is important for policymakers and businesses to carefully consider the economic implications of AGI as it continues to advance.

## Future Directions in AGI Research

As we look towards the future of AGI research, there are several key directions that will shape the development of artificial general intelligence. One of the most important areas of focus will be on enhancing the capabilities of AGI systems to learn and adapt in real-time. This will involve research into advanced machine learning algorithms, neural networks, and reinforcement learning techniques that can enable AGI systems to continually improve their performance and decision-making abilities.

Another crucial direction in AGI research will be the development of more sophisticated natural language processing capabilities. As AGI systems become more integrated into our daily lives, the ability to understand and communicate effectively with humans will be paramount. Research in this area will focus on improving language understanding, generation, and translation capabilities, as well as the development of more intuitive and natural interfaces for interacting with AGI systems.

Furthermore, there will be a continued emphasis on the ethical considerations surrounding the development and deployment of AGI systems. As these technologies become more advanced, it will be essential to ensure that they are used in ways that are beneficial to society and do not cause harm. Research in this area will focus on developing frameworks for ethical AI design, as well as mechanisms for ensuring transparency, accountability, and fairness in AGI systems.

Regulation and governance will also be a critical area of focus in future AGI research. As AGI systems become more powerful and autonomous, there will be a need for regulations and policies that govern their use and ensure that they are used responsibly. Research in this area will focus on developing legal frameworks, standards, and guidelines for the ethical and safe deployment of AGI technologies.

Finally, research in AGI will also need to address the economic impact of these technologies. As AGI systems become more prevalent in industries ranging from healthcare to finance to transportation, there will be significant changes to the job market and economy. Research in this area will focus on understanding the potential impacts of AGI on employment, wages, and economic growth, as well as developing strategies for managing these transitions and ensuring that the benefits of AGI are shared equitably across society.

## Final Thoughts on the Impact of AGI

As we conclude our exploration of Artificial General Intelligence (AGI) and its potential impact on society, it is crucial to reflect on the profound implications that this technology may have on our world. The development of AGI has the potential to revolutionize industries, create new opportunities for innovation, and enhance the quality of life for individuals around the globe. However, with great power comes great responsibility, and it is imperative that we carefully consider the ethical considerations, regulation, and governance surrounding AGI.

One of the most pressing concerns regarding AGI is the ethical implications of creating machines that possess human-like intelligence. As we strive to develop AGI, we must ensure that these systems are designed to prioritize the well-being of humanity and adhere to ethical principles. This includes addressing issues such as bias, privacy, and accountability to ensure that AGI is used for the greater good of society.

In addition to ethical considerations, the regulation and governance of AGI will play a critical role in shaping its impact on society. It is essential that policymakers work alongside industry leaders to establish guidelines and frameworks for the responsible development and deployment of AGI. This includes addressing concerns such as data privacy, cybersecurity, and the potential economic impact of AGI on the workforce.

Furthermore, the technical challenges associated with creating AGI must be carefully considered to ensure that these systems are safe, reliable, and trustworthy.

This includes addressing issues such as robustness, interpretability, and transparency to build confidence in the capabilities of AGI. By overcoming these technical challenges, we can unlock the full potential of AGI and harness its power for the benefit of humanity.

In conclusion, the impact of AGI on society will be far-reaching and transformative. By addressing ethical considerations, regulation and governance, technical challenges, and economic impact, we can pave the way for a future where AGI enhances our lives in meaningful ways. It is up to all stakeholders – from researchers and policymakers to industry leaders and the general public – to work together to ensure that AGI is developed and deployed responsibly for the betterment of society as a whole.

Artificial General Intelligence (AGI) represents a level of artificial intelligence that can understand, learn, and apply knowledge across a wide range of tasks at a human level. Here are some potential use cases for AGI:

1. **Healthcare**
   - **Diagnosis and Treatment Planning**: AGI could diagnose diseases with higher accuracy by analyzing medical data, including patient history, genetic information, and current health metrics. It could also suggest personalized treatment plans.
   - **Drug Discovery**: AGI could accelerate the discovery of new drugs by simulating and predicting the outcomes of molecular interactions and clinical trials.
   - **Robotic Surgery**: Performing complex surgeries with higher precision and minimal human intervention.

2. **Education**
   - **Personalized Learning**: AGI could create custom learning plans for students based on their strengths, weaknesses, and learning styles.
   - **Tutoring and Mentoring**: Providing one-on-one tutoring in any subject, helping students understand complex concepts, and assisting with homework.
   - **Administrative Efficiency**: Automating administrative tasks like grading, scheduling, and resource allocation to allow educators to focus more on teaching.

3. **Business and Finance**
   - **Market Analysis and Trading**: AGI could analyze market trends, financial reports, and economic indicators to make investment decisions or suggest trading strategies.
   - **Customer Service**: Providing highly intelligent and personalized customer support through chatbots and virtual assistants.

- **Business Process Optimization**: Automating and optimizing business processes, from supply chain management to human resource functions.

4. **Environment and Sustainability**
   - **Climate Modeling**: Predicting and mitigating the impacts of climate change through advanced simulation and modeling.
   - **Resource Management**: Efficiently managing natural resources like water, minerals, and energy to minimize waste and promote sustainability.
   - **Environmental Monitoring**: Detecting and responding to environmental hazards such as pollution, deforestation, and natural disasters.

5. **Transportation**
   - **Autonomous Vehicles**: Developing self-driving cars, trucks, and drones that can navigate complex environments and make decisions in real time.
   - **Traffic Management**: Optimizing traffic flow in urban areas to reduce congestion and emissions.
   - **Logistics and Delivery**: Improving the efficiency of logistics networks and delivery systems.

6. **Scientific Research**
   - **Complex Problem Solving**: Tackling problems that require multidisciplinary knowledge and creativity, such as space exploration and quantum physics.
   - **Data Analysis**: Analyzing vast amounts of scientific data to uncover new patterns and insights.
   - **Simulation and Modeling**: Running advanced simulations to test hypotheses and predict outcomes in fields like biology, chemistry, and physics.

7. **Creative Arts**
   - **Content Creation**: Generating music, art, literature, and other forms of creative content.
   - **Design and Innovation**: Assisting in the design of new products, buildings, and technologies by providing innovative ideas and solutions.

- o **Entertainment**: Developing immersive virtual reality experiences, video games, and interactive storytelling.
8. **Security and Defense**
  - o **Threat Detection**: Identifying and responding to cyber threats, physical security risks, and other dangers in real time.
  - o **Strategic Planning**: Assisting in the development of defense strategies and tactics.
  - o **Surveillance and Monitoring**: Automating surveillance systems to detect suspicious activities and respond appropriately.

Developing and utilizing AGI (Artificial General Intelligence) involves a combination of various software tools, frameworks, and platforms. Here are some key types of software and specific examples used in the development and application of AGI:

## Machine Learning and AI Frameworks

1. **TensorFlow**: An open-source machine learning library developed by Google, widely used for building and training neural networks.
2. **PyTorch**: An open-source machine learning library developed by Facebook's AI Research lab, known for its flexibility and ease of use.
3. **Keras**: An open-source software library that provides a Python interface for artificial neural networks, running on top of TensorFlow or Theano.
4. **OpenAI Gym**: A toolkit for developing and comparing reinforcement learning algorithms, providing a wide range of environments.

## Data Processing and Analysis Tools

1. **Pandas**: A data manipulation and analysis library for Python, essential for handling and preprocessing data.
2. **NumPy**: A fundamental package for scientific computing with Python, used for working with arrays and matrices.
3. **Apache Spark**: An open-source distributed computing system used for big data processing and machine learning tasks.

## Natural Language Processing (NLP) Tools

1. **spaCy**: An open-source software library for advanced natural language processing in Python.
2. **NLTK (Natural Language Toolkit)**: A platform for building Python programs to work with human language data.

3. **Hugging Face Transformers**: A library providing pre-trained models for NLP tasks such as text generation, translation, and summarization.

## Reinforcement Learning Platforms

1. **RLLib**: A scalable reinforcement learning library, part of the Ray ecosystem, used for training complex reinforcement learning models.
2. **DeepMind's DQN**: Deep Q-Network, a reinforcement learning algorithm developed by DeepMind, often implemented using TensorFlow or PyTorch.

## Robotics and Simulation Software

1. **ROS (Robot Operating System)**: An open-source framework for writing robot software, providing tools and libraries for building complex robot applications.
2. **Gazebo**: A robot simulation environment that allows for testing and developing robotics algorithms in realistic scenarios.
3. **Unity ML-Agents**: A toolkit for training intelligent agents using reinforcement learning in Unity-based environments.

## Cloud Platforms and Services

1. **Google Cloud AI**: Provides machine learning and AI services, including TensorFlow on Google Cloud, AutoML, and AI Platform for building and deploying models.
2. **AWS AI Services**: Amazon Web Services offers a range of AI services, including SageMaker for building, training, and deploying machine learning models.
3. **Microsoft Azure AI**: Offers AI and machine learning services, including Azure Machine Learning for model training and deployment.

## Development and Collaboration Tools

1. **Jupyter Notebooks**: An open-source web application that allows for creating and sharing documents containing live code, equations, visualizations, and narrative text.
2. **GitHub**: A platform for version control and collaborative software development using Git.
3. **Docker**: A tool designed to make it easier to create, deploy, and run applications by using containers, essential for reproducibility and deployment of AI models.

## Specialized AGI Research Platforms

1. **OpenAI Codex**: An AI system developed by OpenAI that translates natural language into code, part of the broader effort towards AGI.
2. **DeepMind's AlphaZero**: A reinforcement learning algorithm that has achieved superhuman performance in games like chess, shogi, and Go, showcasing the potential of AGI.